THE POETRY OF
NIHONIUM

The Poetry of Nihonium

Walter the Educator

Silent King Books

SILENT KING BOOKS

SKB

Copyright © 2024 by Walter the Educator

All rights reserved. No part of this book may be reproduced in any manner whatsoever without written permission except in the case of brief quotations embodied in critical articles and reviews.

First Printing, 2024

Disclaimer
This book is a literary work; poems are not about specific persons, locations, situations, and/or circumstances unless mentioned in a historical context. This book is for entertainment and informational purposes only. The author and publisher offer this information without warranties expressed or implied. No matter the grounds, neither the author nor the publisher will be accountable for any losses, injuries, or other damages caused by the reader's use of this book. The use of this book acknowledges an understanding and acceptance of this disclaimer.

"Earning a degree in chemistry changed my life!"
- Walter the Educator

dedicated to all the chemistry lovers, like myself, across the world

NIHONIUM

Nihonium emerges, rare and new,

NIHONIUM

A fleeting glimpse in the atomic view,

NIHONIUM

A symphony of particles imbued.

NIHONIUM

In laboratories, where scientists delve,

NIHONIUM

They conjure elements from secrets they unveil,

NIHONIUM

Nihonium, born of fusion's spell,

NIHONIUM

In the alchemy of atoms, it finds its dwell.

NIHONIUM

With atomic number one one thirty, bright,

NIHONIUM

It ventures into realms of scientific light,

NIHONIUM

A fleeting presence in the darkest night,

NIHONIUM

A testament to humanity's curious might.

NIHONIUM

In the heart of stars, where fusion reigns,

NIHONIUM

Nihonium's genesis, a celestial refrain,

NIHONIUM

Forged in the furnace of stellar lanes,

NIHONIUM

It journeys to Earth with enigmatic chains.

NIHONIUM

From synthetic origins, it takes its form,

NIHONIUM

A testament to science's ongoing swarm,

NIHONIUM

With fleeting half-life, it transcends the norm,

NIHONIUM

A tantalizing glimpse of the atomic storm.

NIHONIUM

In the periodic table's sprawling array,

NIHONIUM

Nihonium's presence, a puzzle to assay,

NIHONIUM

It beckons researchers, night and day,

NIHONIUM

To unlock the secrets it holds at bay.

NIHONIUM

With electron clouds in quantum dance,

NIHONIUM

Nihonium whispers secrets in a trance,

NIHONIUM

Its properties a mystery, a cosmic chance,

NIHONIUM

To unravel nature's enigmatic expanse.

NIHONIUM

In laboratories, with precision's might,

NIHONIUM

Scientists probe its properties in the night,

NIHONIUM

Unraveling the mysteries, bit by byte,

NIHONIUM

In the quest for knowledge's guiding light.

NIHONIUM

Nihonium, a testament to human quest,

NIHONIUM

For knowledge, understanding, at our behest,

NIHONIUM

In the dance of atoms, it stands abreast,

NIHONIUM

A symbol of curiosity's eternal zest.

NIHONIUM

So let us celebrate this element rare,

NIHONIUM

In the annals of science, it takes its share,

NIHONIUM

Nihonium, with mysteries to spare,

NIHONIUM

In the cosmic dance, it's a flair.

NIHONIUM

ABOUT THE CREATOR

Walter the Educator is one of the pseudonyms for Walter Anderson. Formally educated in Chemistry, Business, and Education, he is an educator, an author, a diverse entrepreneur, and he is the son of a disabled war veteran. "Walter the Educator" shares his time between educating and creating. He holds interests and owns several creative projects that entertain, enlighten, enhance, and educate, hoping to inspire and motivate you.

Follow, find new works, and stay up to date
with Walter the Educator™
at WaltertheEducator.com

www.ingramcontent.com/pod-product-compliance
Lightning Source LLC
LaVergne TN
LVHW051922060526
838201LV00060B/4129